Twentieth-Century German Verse:
A Selection

ZUR ERMUTIGUNG

So unvermeidbar ein Geschick dir scheine,
Neig ihm dein Haupt in frommer Demut nie.
Was heute sich des Schicksals Maske lieh,
War gestern *vieler* Möglichkeiten *eine*,
Und wird heut ohne dich die Wahl gefällt;—
Von *morgen* die ist dir anheimgestellt.

ENCOURAGEMENT

Let Fate appear however fixed it may,
Bow not your head in meek humility.
What wears today the mask of destiny
Was one of many choices yesterday,
And if today's result seems made without you,
Tomorrow's choices now stand round about you.

—ARTHUR SCHNITZLER: *,,Buch der Sprüche*
und Bedenken"

TWENTIETH-CENTURY

GERMAN

VERSE

A SELECTION TRANSLATED BY

HERMAN SALINGER

Granger Index Reprint Series

BOOKS FOR LIBRARIES PRESS
FREEPORT, NEW YORK

LIBRARY OF CONGRESS CATALOG CARD NUMBER:

68-57065

MANUFACTURED
BY
HALLMARK LITHOGRAPHERS, INC.
IN THE U.S.A.

REMEMBERING

GEORGE MADISON PRIEST

TEACHER · SCHOLAR · TRANSLATOR · FRIEND

25 JANUARY 1873   18 FEBRUARY 1947

HENDERSON, KENTUCKY   PRINCETON, NEW JERSEY

CONTENTS

[ix]

[x]

INTRODUCTION

In presenting this collection, the translator is aware that he has necessarily functioned as an editor. He has, that is, exercised certain rights of selection which, in the aggregate, have shaped the book and given it whatever flavor it has. Not that it would be possible to render a complete accounting of the reasons animating each choice: the act of selection was a response to an appeal, usually a fairly automatic response. It was as if these poems yearned to be reborn in English; the combined result of their yearning and of the translator's compulsive acts of selection makes no pretenses to infallibility. *This book does not pretend to be a grand tour of German poetry in our century.*

On the other hand, it would be a mistake to think of the poems as a random grouping. Practically all of the poets have stature: from Rilke, George, and Hofmannsthal, the great triumvirate, down to Weinheber, Haushofer, and Holthusen. Since, as has been said by Professor A. R. Hohlfeld, every translation is in itself a commentary, further remarks may seem uncalled for. Let me merely transform some part of the commentary implicit in the translations themselves into a few explicit remarks.

These poems will be found to play up and down the scale between the extremes of despair and hope. Poetry, by its very nature, lies between despair and hope: this is the range of the strings of Orpheus. But the phrase can be applied with a peculiar aptness to the poetry of a nation whose greatest poet celebrated emotion as "himmelhoch jauchzend, zum Tode betrübt" (rejoicing to the high heavens, saddened unto death). How especially true this holds for German poetry in an age of crisis such as the first half of this shattered century! And yet, certain poets writing in the German tongue (and this would include the Austrians and, in part, the Bohemian cultural sphere) have made a very real and probably formative contribution to modern poetry. When we start to summarize this contribution, some of its traits seem almost atavistic: a subjectivity—romantically tinged, a sometimes surprising lack of rationalistic approach. In a harsh age, this poetry has remained essentially "naïve" in its values, sincere in sentiment without sentimentality, largely traditional in form and metre, yet highly flexible. That is to say, the folksong and ballad, as modified by Goethe and as sophisticated by Heine, have remained the usual skeletal structure. But there is in evidence, in each of the poets of our collection, a verbal facility which is altogether modern.

It was decided to allow the authors to appear in chronological sequence, according to year of birth. This arrangement has the advantage of simplicity, bringing all the poems of one poet together, but it also involves some disadvantages. In the first place, contemporaries may have no other closeness than the chronological one, so that some of the juxtapositions in this book may appear unmotivated. Furthermore, the present arrangement (although the most satisfactory hit upon) necessarily contradicts some of the salient facts of influence and "importance." For example, it is necessary to place as important and influential a poet as Rainer Maria Rilke fairly early in the collection because he was born in 1875, whereas a minor poet like Heinrich Lersch, of less lasting influence, appears farther toward the end of the *personae*. Lersch died ten years after Rilke, yet today, a decade and a half later, it is the earlier and, of course, greater poet whose influence is the determining one, a quarter of a century beyond the grave, and whose personality and work remain the center of scholarly inquiry and literary attention—and are likely to remain so for many more years. These factors have been taken into account by the inclusion of a larger selection from the poems of Rilke and of one or two others who have exerted a really powerful influence on contemporary society as well as contemporary verse.

My reason for offering more translations from the already extensively translated poet Rilke may require no further apologia. If further justification be needed, it will be found that at least two of the poems are from his early work, seldom accorded any representation in English, one is a very late poem, written at Muzot two years before his death. Several are—so far as I can ascertain—not previously translated. Of the others I can only say that I love them in the original sufficiently to be unwilling to do without them in any personal collection. And yet I have not been satisfied by any of their previous reincarnations in English.

If Isolde Kurz was less known for her poetry than for her stories (she is included here for that feminine blend of the romantic with the matter-of-fact that marks her as part of the transition to naturalism), it must be admitted that the author of the little verse which stands as an epigraph to the collection, Arthur Schnitzler (1862-1931), is scarcely remembered as a poet at all, although his continuing importance to the Austrian drama can scarcely be overrated. Of the others, each has his or her *raison d'être* in this collection. Two poems by Stefan George were chosen in order to illustrate the twin phases of lyricist and prophet. His extraordinary poetic qualities have already been introduced to the American public *in extenso* through the Valhope-Morwitz translation (1943) and its further elaborations and extensions under the imprint of the University of North Carolina Press. The tragedy of George's misappropriation by Dr. Goebbels has not diminished his right to a place here or elsewhere; rather, it makes a careful reading of the bardistic second poem all the more imperative. The satiric fantasy of Christian Morgenstern, little known in this country but sometimes more or less adequately characterized as a kind of German Lewis Carroll—or a distant literary cousin—marks him as a member of that generation of the middle seventies which included Rilke, Hofmannsthal, Thomas Mann, and Herman Hesse, insofar as his imaginative "escapism" reveals his own individual form of artistic *isolement*. An intellectual to his fingertips, he wrapped himself in a cloak of strange, almost geometrical humor, which, along with his serious lyrics and aphorisms, succeeded in temporarily veiling his meaning from the crowd. Much could be said of Hugo von Hofmannsthal, but I have here chosen, as single representative of his work (and because of personal appeal), a balladesque narrative (reminiscent of his verse dramas) which is neo-romantic in tone, inward in direction, and deeply characteristic of the poet's psyche. This poem gives us Hofmannsthal in his endless preoccupation with the past: Europe's, Austria's, and his own, more succinctly summarized through the figure of his own grandmother than almost anywhere else, perhaps, in so short a compass.

The poems of Hermann Claudius have always had, for me, a haunting lyric charm; the melodic cadences—especially of "Der Rosenbusch"—have never left my inner hearing for very long since they first lodged there more than a dozen years ago. To a somewhat lesser degree, Ricarda

Huch has left a lasting mark on the translator's memory. She has for decades been so much a part of every anthology in her homeland that she would be missed here. The theme of "Tief in den Himmel verklingt" has, moreover, an especial, almost topical appeal. The rather extensive lyric work of Hans Carossa is represented by one small gem, typical of his classic craftsmanship and—if the terms still have any validity—romantic approach to human values. Of the older generation, he has really screened those values through the medium of the science and literature, the religion and philosophy, in short the classic-romantic tradition best summed up by the expression *Goethezeit*.

Rudolf Binding's controlled expression of a disciplined emotion contrasts with Ina Seidel's thoroughly feminine outlook upon the same emotion. Agnes Miegel's artfully folkloristic ballad objectifies the maternal instinct; her poem acts almost like an extroversion of instinct when compared with the deeply personal tone of Franz Werfel's egocentric early lyric. I include the latter here partly because Edith Abercrombie Snow passed it by—possibly as too romantic—in her generally good renditions of Werfel (Princeton University Press, 1945) and also because Werfel, though famous for the expressionism so often evident in his verse, did not always limit himself exclusively to the technique of that school. The expressionist trend is felt again in Georg Trakl's "Nocturne," to some extent in Ernst Wiechert's religious introversion, and in Josef Weinheber's interior landscape.

In the impassioned lines of Heinrich Lersch and in Max Barthel's finely etched vignette of "The Plow" we are glad to rediscover the now sometimes forgotten broad internationalism and deep pacifism of the post World War I poetic

clan of "worker-poets" (*Arbeiter-Dichter*). We may feel
some doubt of its actual contemporary presence until we
meet it again in the newer poet, Ulrich Becher. After the
prison-pallor and despair of Albrecht Haushofer, anti-
Hitler son of the geopolitician Karl Haushofer, comes
Becher's more sanguine activism. A middle way is offered,
to those who are receptive to it, by the simple wisdom of
Hermann Hesse. Awarded the Nobel Prize for literature in
1947, at the age of seventy, but never really known in our
hemisphere as a lyric poet, Hesse the novelist had for a mat-
ter of decades combatted nationalistic narrowness with the
broad human and humanist sympathy of a true poet. His
philosophy, personally arrived at, remains—at least as we
may glimpse it in these poetic selections—a highly per-
sonalized one.

Hans Egon Holthusen's is one of the most clearly sig-
nificant voices in the lyric literature of mid-century Ger-
many. Definitely in the traditional current of German
poetry that derived new impetus from Rilke, Holthusen
draws from fresh springs of an inspiration all his own. His
particular awareness is peculiarly modern; eddies and cross-
currents from W. H. Auden and the later work of Eliot are
discernible, but I am not yet as much convinced of their
inner importance as are some of the present-day critics. In
Holthusen's performance I still hear, through the disso-
nances of grief and war and atomic anxieties, the major
chords of German individualism and idealism. Of the Ger-
man-speaking peoples the words of the wordly-wise Aus-
trian playwright Arthur Schnitzler, which appear on our
title page, are even more true today than they were a gen-
eration ago.

Grinnell College,   H. S.
Grinnell, Iowa
3 February 1952

ACKNOWLEDGMENTS

For permission to reprint the original texts of the poems and to publish my own translations of them, I wish to thank several German, Austrian and Swiss publishing houses and certain individual poets or their heirs. These include: The Rainer Wunderlich Verlag Hermann Leins of Tübingen and, specifically, Dr. A. Christiansen of that firm, for the poem by Isolde Kurz; the Insel-Verlag and, more specifically, its *Zweigstelle* Wiesbaden, for Ricarda Huch's poem (from her final collection, *Herbstfeuer*, which appeared in the Insel-Bücherei, 1944), for the various poems by Rilke, Morgenstern and Carossa, in which connection I am also indebted to the directors of the Rilke-Archive, to Frau Margareta Morgenstern and to Dr. Hans Carossa. At the same time I should like to express very particular thanks to Dr. Friedrich Michael of the Wiesbaden editorial office of Insel-Verlag for his encouragement, assistance and cooperation in locating other publishers: a difficult and involved task for me during the post-war period. Thus I am able to thank the Hans Dulk Verlag, Hamburg and the heirs and literary executor of Rudolf G. Binding for permission to reprint and translate his poem; the Lothar Blanvalet Verlag, Berlin-Wannsee, for permission to use and translate the two sonnets by Albrecht Haushofer taken from *Moabiter Sonette* published by that firm; Otto Müller, Salzburg, Austria for the use of Georg Trakl's "Romanze zur Nacht" from Volume One of Trakl's Collected Works (*Die Dichtungen*) published by that firm; the Eugen Diederichs Verlag, Düsseldorf-Köln, and, in particular, Dr. Peter Diederichs, for Agnes Miegel's poem; the heirs of Ernst Wiechert and the Verlag Kurt Desch, München, for "Ein Kind hat geweint"; the Verlag Helmut Küpper (formerly Georg Bondi), München, and Helmut Küpper himself, as well as Dr. Robert Boehringer of Geneva, Switzerland, the literary executor and biographer of Stefan George, for the two George poems and for approval of my translations; the S. Fischer Verlag, Frankfurt am Main, and Dr. Gottfried Bermann Fischer personally for his part in permitting use of the poems by Werfel and Hofmannsthal; furthermore, Pantheon Books, Inc., New York, and the Bollingen Foundation for the Hofmannsthal poem, as well as Mrs. Alma Mahler Werfel and Professor Gustave O. Arlt (of the University of California at Los Angeles) in connection with the poem by Franz Werfel; for the poem by Heinrich Lersch, his widow Frau Lersch and the Deutsche Verlags-Anstalt, G.m.b.H., Stuttgart, who originally published the volume containing it (*Mit brüderlicher Stimme*, by Heinrich Lersch, 1934); again, the Deutsche Verlags-Anstalt, Stuttgart, for "Ehe" by Ina Seidel (from *Gedichte*, 1937, published by that firm); to Dr. H. Wegener and the Hoffmann und Campe Verlag, Hamburg, as well as to Frau Weinheber, for the poem by Josef Weinheber.

I have, moreover, an even closer personal debt of gratitude to several of these poets themselves with whom I have been in cordial and heart-warming correspondence. These include Hermann Hesse of Montagnola, Tessin, Switzerland (he and his publishers, Fretz & Wasmuth Verlag of Zürich, have been generous and cooperative); Max Barthel of Niederbreisig am Rhein and Hermann Claudius, Hamburg-Hummelsbüttel, both of whom have generously sent me some of their recent lyrics;[1] Dr. Hans Egon Holthusen

[1] All three poems by Hermann Claudius appear in the volume *Und weiter wachsen Gott und Welt*, copyright 1936 by Albert Langen-Georg Müller Verlag, G.m.b.H., München.

of München, with whom I have had a most interesting exchange of letters;[2] and Ulrich Becher, who alternates between Basel, Switzerland and Vienna.[3] I am happy to include a friend of long standing, Professor Henry Schnitzler of the University of California at Los Angeles, who willingly permitted the use of his father's poem on our title page,[4] though regretting the necessary exclusion of the adjective Austrian from the title of the collection—not without the translator's regrets as well.

Certain of my translations have previously appeared in print. For permission to reprint these I must thank the editors of *Poet Lore* (Boston), *Fantasy* (Pittsburgh), *Monatshefte für deutschen Unterricht* (Madison, Wisconsin), *Accent* (Urbana, Illinois) and *Books Abroad* (University of Oklahoma Press, Norman, Oklahoma).

[2] Dr. Holthusen's poems are taken from the collection *Hier in der Zeit*, published and copyright 1949 by R. Piper & Co. Verlag, München.

[3] Herr Becher's poem, copyright by himself, is from the collection *Reise zum blauen Tag*, Verlag Buchdruckerei Volksstimme St. Gallen, 1946.

[4] Arthur Schnitzler's *Buch der Sprüche und Bedenken*, containing, among its highly original and characteristic prose, a very few verse aphorisms such as "Zur Ermutigung," was copyright 1927 by Phaidon-Verlag, Wien.

TRANSLATOR'S NOTE

IT has been my endeavor to preserve the thought-content of the original poems, as well as their original form, intact; barring this, to give the poems what seemed an equivalent form in our prosody. Spelling and punctuation vary with the authors; there has been no effort to normalize them. Critical apparatus, biographical and bibliographical data have been dispensed with as not adding appreciably to the enjoyment of the poetry. In most cases, such information will be readily accessible to anyone desiring to track it down.

Permission to reprint originals and translations is acknowledged elsewhere.

To my former colleague, Dr. William H. Rey, now of the University of Washington, I am grateful for counsel and assistance. To my brother, David L. Salinger, my thanks are due for two of the three Christian Morgenstern translations, since we did "The Pike" together during a fishing trip and "The Impossible Fact" conjointly by mail. Out of discussions with my good friend Dr. Arthur R. Schultz of Wesleyan University grew the writing of the Introduction, whose better parts he inspired. My former colleague at Grinnell, Dr. Marina Farmakis, has done her best to help with revisions and proofreading. Miss Miriam Brokaw of the Princeton University Press has been an understanding and patient co-worker. The original idea of collecting my translations, however, stems from my wife; without her, the book would never have taken shape.

H. S.

Twentieth-Century German Verse:
A Selection

ISOLDE KURZ

Die erste Nacht

Jetzt kommt die Nacht, die erste Nacht im Grab.
Oh, wo ist aller Glanz, der dich umgab?
In kalter Erde ist dein Bett gemacht.
Wie wirst du schlummern diese Nacht?
Vom letzten Regen ist dein Kissen feucht.
Nachtvögel schrein, vom Wind emporgescheucht.
Kein Lämpchen brennt dir mehr, nur kalt und fahl
spielt auf der Schlummerstatt der Mondenstrahl.
Die Stunden schleichen. Schläfst du bis zum Tag?
Horchst du wie ich auf jeden Glockenschlag?
Wie kann ich ruhn und schlummern kurze Frist,
wenn du, mein Lieb, so schlecht gebettet bist?

ISOLDE KURZ

The First Night

Now night comes on, your first night in the grave.
Oh where is all your gleam and all your light?
In the cold earth is laid the bed you have.
How will you slumber, o my dear, tonight?
From the last rain your pillow still is wet.
The night-birds cry. The winds rise up and race.
No lamp burns for you, only moonbeams fret
their pattern on your grassy slumber-place.
The hours creep. And will you sleep till dawn?
Or hear like me each striking hour move on?
How can sleep fold my eyes or wrap my head,
with you, my dear, so badly brought to bed?

RICARDA HUCH

Tief in den Himmel . . .

Tief in den Himmel verklingt
Traurig der letzte Stern,
Noch eine Nachtigall singt
Fern,—fern.
Geh schlafen, mein Herz, es ist Zeit.
Kühl weht die Ewigkeit.

Matt im Schoß liegt die Hand,
Einst so tapfer am Schwert.
War, wofür du entbrannt,
Kampfes wert?
Geh schlafen, mein Herz, es ist Zeit.
Kühl weht die Ewigkeit.

RICARDA HUCH

Deep in the Heavens

Deep in the heavens grows pale
Sadly one final star;
Still sings a nightingale
Far,—far.
It is time to slumber, my soul.
Eternity blows cool.

In the lap, the hand lies tamed
That held the sword tight.
Was all for which you flamed
Worthy the fight?
It is time to slumber, my soul.
Eternity blows cool.

RUDOLF G. BINDING

Liebe

Nun stehn die Hirsche still auf dunklen Schneisen,
die Löwen stehen still im Felsentor;
nun schweigen Nachtigallen ihrer Weisen
und Sterne, Sterne hören auf zu kreisen
und aus den Sonnen tritt kein Tag hervor.

In gleiche Nacht sind wir nun eingetaucht,
in gleichen Tag und wieder Tag und Nacht,
ein gleiches Sterben hat uns angehaucht,
zwei Leben sind im Augenblick verraucht
und gleiches Wissen hat uns stumm gemacht.

Es ist als ob die Welt sanft von uns wich—
Die Löwen stehen still im Felsentor
und Sterne, Sterne—Mond und Stern verblich
und alles starb, als du und ich
und ich und du sich Herz in Herz verlor.

RUDOLF G. BINDING

Love Song

The deer stand still now in the darkened forest;
the lions stand in the cavern's rocky mouth.
The nightingales that here together chorused
are silent and the stars stop circling o'er us
and from the suns no morrow issues forth.

In equal night together we go down,
in equal day, in equal day and night.
An equal death upon us both has blown
its breath, and like a smoke our lives have flown
and equal is our silence at the sight.

As if the world away from us were turned—
the lions stand in the cavern's mouth like rocks—
like candles, star and moon away have burned,
and all has died except our hearts that yearned.
And firm each heart upon the other locks.

STEFAN GEORGE

Nach der Lese

(AUS ,,DAS JAHR DER SEELE'')

Wir schreiten auf und ab im reichen flitter
Des buchenganges beinah bis zum tore
Und sehen außen in dem feld vom gitter
Den mandelbaum zum zweitenmal im flore.

Wir suchen nach den schattenfreien bänken
Dort wo uns niemals fremde stimmen scheuchten·
In träumen unsre arme sich verschränken·
Wir laben uns am langen milden leuchten

Wir fühlen dankbar wie zu leisem brausen
Von wipfeln strahlenspuren auf uns tropfen
Und blicken nur und horchen wenn in pausen
Die reifen früchte an den boden klopfen.

STEFAN GEORGE

After Harvest

(FROM "THE YEAR OF THE SOUL")

We stride together in the rich brocade
of broken sunlight almost to the gate
under the beech-trees down the long arcade
to watch the almond's second blossoming, late.

We look for benches shadow-free in streams
of sun where strangers' voices never fright us.
Our arms are intertwined as in our dreams.
We drink the mellow afternoons that light us.

And when the autumn wind, soft and sublime,
nips at the treetops, sunbeams tilt and pour
upon us and we hear from time to time
the ripe fruits thud against the orchard floor.

STEFAN GEORGE

Aus „Der Stern des Bundes"

Aus purpurgluten sprach des himmels zorn:
Mein blick ist abgewandt von diesem volk . . .
Siech ist der geist! tot ist die tat!
Nur sie die nach dem heiligen bezirk
Geflüchtet sind auf goldenen triremen
Die meine harfen spielen und im tempel
Die opfer tun . . . und die den weg noch suchend
Brünstig die arme in den abend strecken
Nur deren schritten folg ich noch mit huld—
Und aller rest ist nacht und nichts.

STEFAN GEORGE

From "The Star of the Covenant"

In purple fire spoke the heavenly wrath:
My countenance is turned from these, this folk . . .
Sick is the spirit! dead is the deed!
Only those few who to the holy place
took flight in golden triremes and who play
my harps and psalteries and in the temple
the sacrifices render . . . and who search,
burningly stretching arms into the evening,
only their steps I follow still with grace—
And all the rest is night and naught.

CHRISTIAN MORGENSTERN

Der Hecht

Ein Hecht, vom heiligen Antōn
bekehrt, beschloß, samt Frau und Sohn,
am vegetarischen Gedanken
moralisch sich emporzuranken.

Er aß seit jenem nur noch dies:
Seegras, Seerose und Seegries.
Doch Gries, Gras, Rose floß, o Graus,
entsetzlich wieder hinten aus.

Der ganze Teich ward angesteckt.
Fünfhundert Fische sind verreckt.
Doch Sankt Antōn, gerufen eilig,
sprach nichts als: Heilig! heilig! heilig!

CHRISTIAN MORGENSTERN

The Pike

A pike, converted by the Saint
Antonius, abjured the taint
of all but vegetable diet
and swore his wife and son would try it.

He ate, in this new moral status,
lake grass, lake grits, and lake potatoes.
But grass, grits, spuds all sped (o spite)
aft something awful out of sight.

Thus all the pond was putrefied.
Five hundred fellow-fishes died.
The Saint, when summoned, answered slowly
nothing but: Holy! Holy! Holy!

CHRISTIAN MORGENSTERN

Die unmögliche Tatsache

Palmström, etwas schon an Jahren,
wird an einer Straßenbeuge
und von einem Kraftfahrzeuge
überfahren.

„Wie war" (spricht er, sich erhebend
und entschlossen weiterlebend)
„möglich, wie dies Unglück, ja—:
daß es überhaupt geschah?

„Ist die Staatskunst anzuklagen
in Bezug auf Kraftfahrwagen?
Gab die Polizeivorschrift
hier dem Fahrer freie Trift?

„Oder war vielmehr verboten,
hier Lebendige zu Toten
umzuwandeln,—kurz und schlicht:
D u r f t e hier der Kutscher nicht—?"

Eingehüllt in feuchte Tücher,
prüft er die Gesetzesbücher
und ist alsobald im Klaren:
Wagen durften dort nicht fahren!

Und er kommt zu dem Ergebnis:
Nur ein Traum war das Erlebnis.
Weil, so schließt er messerscharf,
nicht sein k a n n, was nicht sein d a r f.

CHRISTIAN MORGENSTERN

The Impossible Fact

Palmström, now no longer so
young as once, is by a stray
motor vehicle one day
laid low.

"How," he said (he firmly chose
to go on living) as he rose,
"was it possible, pray tell,
that this contretemps befell?

"Must we blame our Statecraft's role
regarding Motor Car Control?
Did the Ordinance, let us say,
give that Driver Right-of-Way?

"Contrariwise, could Law have said
to change the Quick into the Dead
was here forbid? To be quite clear:
had that Chauffeur no Business here?"

Shrouded in wet Applications,
searching through the Regulations,
he finds at last an Answer graphic:
that Place, in fact, was Closed-to-Traffic!

So Palmström comes to this Conclusion:
his Adventure was Illusion,
since, he argues reasonably,
that *can* not be which *must* not be.

CHRISTIAN MORGENSTERN

Die Oste

Er ersann zur Weste
eines Nachts die Oste!
Sprach: „Was es auch koste!—"
sprach (mit großer Geste):

„Laßt uns auch von hinten
seidne Hyazinthen
samt Karfunkelknöpfen
unsern Rumpf umkröpfen!
Nicht nur auf dem Magen
laßt uns Uhren tragen,
nicht nur überm Herzen
unsre Sparsesterzen!
Fort mit dem betreßten
Privileg der Westen!
Gleichheit allerstücken!
Osten für den Rücken!"

Und sieh da, kein Schneider
sagte hierzu: Leider—!
Hunderttausend Scheren
sah man Stoffe queren . . .
Ungezählte Posten
wurden schönster Osten
noch vor seinem Tode
„letzter Schrei" der Mode.

The Eastcoat

To accompany the waistcoat,
he invented, before sleeping,
"At all costs!" (with gesture sweeping)
he invented him an eastcoat:

"Let us *en derrière* evince
silk and satin hyacinths,
clasp carbuncle buttons, buckles
rumpwards on our dorsal knuckles!
Not alone o'er bulging entrail
wear our watches, strictly ventral,
spread not only, proudly breasted,
our treasured ducats. Down with vested
privilege, long hedged and hoarded,
befrogged, bebraided and becorded!
Equality no garb shall lack!
Long live eastcoats for the back!"

And see: no tailor—man nor boss—
says, "I'm sorry, but I fear . . ."
By the thousand, shear on shear
cuts the various cloth across . . .
In a thousand towns, at least,
the extremely novel east-
coat becomes, ere his demise,
the stylish cynosure of eyes.

HUGO VON HOFMANNSTHAL

Großmutter und Enkel

„Ferne ist dein Sinn, dein Fuß
Nur in meiner Tür!"
Woher weißt dus gleich beim Gruß?
„Kind, weil ich es spür."

Was? „Wie Sie aus süßer Ruh
Süß durch dich erschrickt."—
Sonderbar, wie S i e hast du
Vor dich hingenickt.

„Einst . . ." Nein: jetzt im Augenblick!
Mich beglückt der Schein—
„Kind, was haucht dein Wort und Blick
Jetzt in mich hinein?

Meine Mädchenzeit voll Glanz
Mit verstohlnem Hauch
Öffnet mir die Seele ganz!"
Ja, ich spür es auch:

Und ich bin bei dir und bin
Wie auf fremdem Stern:
Ihr und dir mit wachem Sinn
Schwankend nah und fern!

„Als ich dem Großvater dein
Mich fürs Leben gab,
Trat ich so verwirrt nicht ein
Wie nun in mein Grab."

Grab? Was redest du von dem?
Das ist weit von dir!

HUGO VON HOFMANNSTHAL

Grandmother and Grandson

"Your mind is far, however light
  your footstep on my sill!"
How can you know at once, on sight?
  "Child, I feel it well."

Feel what? "How She begins to stir,
  wakes sweetly from sweet sleep."
Strange! you looked just now like her,
  straight at me and deep.

"Once—" No, now: a moment past!
  And I found it good—
"Child, what thoughts of yours take fast,
  breathed into my blood?

"All my girlhood gleam and spark,
  with a secret kiss,
lifts my soul from age and dark!"
  Yes, I too feel this:

I am here, yet as I were
  on a distant star:
now with you and now with her,
  swaying near and far.

"When my young lips spoke the vow
  to Grandfather I gave,
I was less confused than now,
  going to my grave."

Grave? Why do you speak of *it*
  in this hour of cheer?

[19]

Sitzest plaudernd und bequem
Mit dem Enkel hier.

Deine Augen frisch und reg,
Deine Wangen hell—
„Flog nicht übern kleinen Weg
Etwas schwarz und schnell?"

Etwas ist, das wie im Traum
Mich Verliebten hält.
Wie der enge schwüle Raum
Seltsam mich umstellt!

„Fühlst du, was jetzt mich umblitzt
Und mein stockend Herz?
Wenn du bei dem Mädchen sitzt,
Unter Kuß und Scherz,

„Fühl es fort und denk an mich,
Aber ohne Graun:
Denk, wie ich im Sterben glich
Jungen, jungen Fraun."

Chatting cozily you sit
  with your grandson here.

Your brow is smooth, your two eyes laugh,
  your cheeks like roses glow—
"Did I see something by that path,
  black and busy, go?"

There is something dreamlike holds
  the lover that is me.
How this sultry room enfolds
  me endearingly!

"Do you feel the flash and swirl
  around my stuttering breast?—
When you sit beside your girl,
  kiss her, closely pressed.

"Feel it still. And fearless, think,
  though I am not there:
how *like* I was, on this last brink,
  to women: young and fair."

RAINER MARIA RILKE

Ich war ein Kind

Ich war ein Kind und träumte viel
und hatte noch nicht Mai;
da trug ein Mann sein Saitenspiel
an unserm Hof vorbei.
Da hab ich bange aufgeschaut:
„O Mutter, laß mich frei . . ."
  Bei seiner Laute erstem Laut
  brach etwas mir entzwei.

Ich wußte, eh sein Sang begann:
Es wird mein Leben sein.
Sing nicht, sing nicht, du fremder Mann:
Es wird mein Leben sein.

Du singst mein Glück und meine Müh,
mein Lied singst du und dann:
mein Schicksal singst du viel zu früh,
so daß ich, wie ich blüh und blüh
es nie mehr leben kann.

Er sang. Und dann verklang sein Schritt,—
er mußte weiterziehn;
und sang mein Lied, das ich nie litt,
und sang mein Glück, das mir entglitt,
und nahm mich mit und nahm mich mit—
und keiner weiß wohin . . .

RAINER MARIA RILKE

I Was a Child

I was a child when dreams begin
and had not reached my May;
a wanderer with a violin
passed by our door one day.
I saw him coming and I cried:
"O Mother, let me go . . ."
Something shattered deep inside
at the first stroke of his bow.

I knew before his song began:
this, this will be my life.
O do not sing, you unknown man:
for this will be my life.
You sing the joy, the pain of me,
you sing my song and then
sing much too soon: my destiny;
no matter what my blossoming be,
I shall not live it again.

He sang. His footsteps rang and died—
far he had to fare;
he sang the burden I never bore
and sang the rose I never wore
and took me with him far and wide—
and nobody knows where . . .

RAINER MARIA RILKE

Wenn die Uhren so nah ...

Wenn die Uhren so nah
wie im eigenen Herzen schlagen,
und die Dinge mit zagen
Stimmen sich fragen:
Bist du da?—:

dann bin ich nicht der, der am Morgen erwacht,
einen Namen schenkt mir die Nacht,
den keiner, den ich am Tage sprach,
ohne tiefes Fürchten erführe—

Jede Türe
in mir gibt nach . . .

Und da weiß ich, daß nichts vergeht,
keine Geste und kein Gebet
(dazu sind die Dinge zu schwer),
meine ganze Kindheit steht
immer um mich her.
Niemals bin ich allein.
Viele, die vor mir lebten
und fort von mir strebten,
webten,
webten
an meinem Sein.

Und setz ich mich zu dir her
und sage dir leise: Ich litt—
hörst du?

Wer weiß wer
murmelt es mit.

RAINER MARIA RILKE
When the Clocks Strike

When the clocks strike so near
they strike in my very heart,
and things tremble and start
and ask each other in fear:
Are you here?—

then I am not he, who saw morning's light;
a name is given me at night:
a name that no one I spoke to by day
could hear without a fear that is great—

Every gate
in me gives way . . .

Then I know that nothing dies or disbands:
no wave of hands nor prayer of hands
(all things are too heavy, too solid and wide);
my entire childhood stands
always at my side.
I am never alone.
Many (my life had not begun),
that far from me run,
spun,
spun
my being and bone.

And when I come and sit near
and say: "I suffered" to you—
"do you hear?"

    Who knows who
    murmurs it too.

RAINER MARIA RILKE

Der Tod ist groß

Der Tod ist groß.
Wir sind die Seinen
lachenden Munds.
Wenn wir uns mitten im Leben meinen
wagt er zu weinen
mitten in uns.

RAINER MARIA RILKE
Death Is Great

Death is great.
We are his people
who smile and jest.
When we deem ourselves steeped in life deep,
he dares to weep
deep in our breast.

RAINER MARIA RILKE

Die Erblindende

Sie saß so wie die anderen beim Tee.
Mir war zuerst, als ob sie ihre Tasse
ein wenig anders als die andern fasse.
Sie lächelte einmal. Es tat fast weh.

Und als man schließlich sich erhob und sprach
und langsam und wie es der Zufall brachte
durch viele Zimmer ging (man sprach und lachte),
da sah ich sie. Sie ging den andern nach,

verhalten, so wie eine, welche gleich
wird singen müssen und vor vielen Leuten;
auf ihren hellen Augen, die sich freuten,
war Licht von außen wie auf einem Teich.

Sie folgte langsam, und sie brauchte lang,
als wäre etwas noch nicht überstiegen;
und doch: als ob, nach einem Übergang,
sie nicht mehr gehen würde, sondern fliegen.

RAINER MARIA RILKE
Going Blind

She sat just like the other ones at tea.
At first it seemed to me she lifted up
not quite the way the others did, her cup.
And once she smiled: a smile it hurt to see.

And when they stood and chatted by their chairs
and slowly, quite as chance might have it, walked
through all those many rooms (they laughed and talked),
I saw her follow as they went in pairs.

She was withdrawn, like one who waits beyond
a turn of time, to sing before a crowd;
upon her clear eyes (happy, almost proud)
light fell as if from outside on a pond.

She followed slowly, and she felt her way,
as though she still must overcome some thing;
and yet, as if, after a certain day,
her steps would lift and lighten and take wing.

RAINER MARIA RILKE

Eva

Einfach steht sie an der Kathedrale
großem Aufstieg, nah der Fensterrose,
mit dem Apfel in der Apfelpose,
schuldlos-schuldig ein für alle Male

an dem Wachsenden, das sie gebar,
seit sie aus dem Kreis der Ewigkeiten
liebend fortging, um sich durchzustreiten
durch die Erde, wie ein junges Jahr.

Ach, sie hätte gern in jenem Land
noch ein wenig weilen mögen, achtend
auf der Tiere Eintracht und Verstand.

Doch da sie den Mann entschlossen fand,
ging sie mit ihm, nach dem Tode trachtend,
und sie hatte Gott noch kaum gekannt.

RAINER MARIA RILKE

Eva

Simply she stands, by the cathedral portal
over its arch and near the window's rose,
with the apple in the apple pose,
forever guiltless-guilty of the mortal

growing thing she thus had brought to birth
when from the eternal circle wide
she went forth loving, now to strive and stride
like a young year walking through the earth.

Ah! in that land she could have wished to stay
yet for a while among the beasts whose breath
breathed peace and understanding of their way.

But when she found the Man determined, they
went, she with him, turning her face toward death;
and she had known God like a passing day.

RAINER MARIA RILKE

Der Goldschmied

Warte! Langsam! droh ich jedem Ringe
und vertröste jedes Kettenglied:
später, draußen, kommt das, was geschieht.
Dinge, sag ich, Dinge, Dinge, Dinge!
wenn ich schmiede; vor dem Schmied
hat noch keines irgendwas zu sein
oder ein Geschick auf sich zu laden.
Hier sind alle gleich, von Gottes Gnaden:
ich, das Gold, das Feuer und der Stein.

Ruhig, ruhig, ruf nicht so, Rubin!
Diese Perle leidet, und es fluten
Wassertiefen im Aquamarin.
Dieser Umgang mit euch Ausgeruhten
ist ein Schrecken: alle wacht ihr auf!
Wollt ihr Bläue blitzen? Wollt ihr bluten?
Ungeheuer funkelt mir der Hauf.

Und das Gold, es scheint mit mir verständigt;
in der Flamme hab ich es gebändigt,
aber reizen muß ichs um den Stein.
Und auf einmal, um den Stein zu fassen,
schlägt das Raubding mit metallnem Hassen
seine Krallen in mich selber ein.

RAINER MARIA RILKE
The Goldsmith

Slowly! Patience! I remind the rings
and console and calm each chain-link with:
outside, later, life begins its myth.
Things, I say, things, things, things!
when I work with them; before the smith
no thing has to be a thing alone
or to wear a fate upon its face.
Here all are alike, by God's good grace:
I, the gold, the fire, and the stone.

Quiet, ruby, do not call so loud.
This pearl is pained, and see how through and through
under aquamarine the quick tides crowd.
This living with the mystery in you
is stony terror: all shake off your sleep!
Eager to bleed? Eager to blaze out blue?
Monstrously flares up at me: the heap.

And the gold seems docile now and tame;
I have mastered it utterly, I and the flame.
Still I must entice it round the stone.
Then to hold the stone fast, suddenly,
the thing of prey with a metallic glee
strikes its claws into my flesh and bone.

RAINER MARIA RILKE

Spaziergang

Schon ist mein Blick am Hügel, dem besonnten,
dem Wege, den ich kaum begann, voran.
So faßt uns das, was wir nicht fassen konnten,
voller Erscheinung aus der Ferne an—

und wandelt uns, auch wenn wirs nicht erreichen,
in jenes, das wir, kaum es ahnend, sind;
ein Zeichen weht, erwidernd unserm Zeichen . . .
Wir aber spüren nur den Gegenwind.

RAINER MARIA RILKE

Walk

My eyes already touch that hill, sun-gold,
ending the path I've scarcely started. We're
thus gripped by what we could not grasp and hold,
full of its immanence when far from here—

and changed by it, though never reaching there,
into those selves, scarce guessing, we conceal:
a sign waves, answering the sign we bear . . .
And yet the counterwind is all we feel.

RAINER MARIA RILKE

O sage, Dichter . . .

O sage, Dichter, was du tust?—Ich rühme.
Aber das Tödliche und Ungetüme,
wie hältst du's aus, wie nimmst du's hin?—Ich rühme.
Aber das Namenlose, Anonyme,
wie rufst du's, Dichter, dennoch an?—Ich rühme.
Woher dein Recht, in jeglichem Kostüme,
in jeder Maske wahr zu sein?—Ich rühme.
Und daß das Stille und das Ungestüme
wie Stern und Sturm dich kennen?:—weil ich rühme.

RAINER MARIA RILKE
O Tell Us, Poet . . .

O tell us, poet, what you do.—I praise.
Yes, but the *deadly* and the *monstrous* phase,
how do you take it, how resist?—I praise.
But the anonymous, the nameless maze,
how summon it, how call it, poet?—I praise.
What right is yours, in all these varied ways,
under a thousand masks yet true?—I praise.
And why do stillness and the roaring blaze,
both star and storm acknowledge you?—because
                                        I praise.

HERMANN HESSE

Jugendflucht

Der müde Sommer senkt das Haupt
Und schaut sein falbes Bild im See.
Ich wandle müde und bestaubt
Im Schatten der Allee.

Durch Pappeln geht ein zager Wind.
Der Himmel hinter mir ist rot,
Und vor mir Abendängste sind
—Und Dämmerung—und Tod.

Ich wandle müde und bestaubt,
Und hinter mir bleibt zögernd stehn
Die Jugend, neigt das schöne Haupt
Und will nicht fürder mit mir gehn.

HERMANN HESSE

Youth's Flight

The tired summer sinks its head,
sees its pale picture in the pond.
I wander tired, in dust and dread,
the shadowy avenue beyond.

Through poplars strays a timid wind.
The sky behind me now is red,
with evening fears, with daylight thinned,
twilight and death ahead.

I wander tired, in dust and dread.
Behind me, youth stops wistfully,
lowering his lovely head,
and would no longer walk with me.

HERMANN HESSE

Manchmal

Manchmal, wenn ein Vogel ruft
Oder ein Wind geht in den Zweigen
Oder ein Hund bellt im fernsten Gehöft,
Dann muß ich lange lauschen und schweigen.

Meine Seele flieht zurück,
Bis wo vor tausend vergessenen Jahren
Der Vogel und der wehende Wind
Mir ähnlich und meine Brüder waren.

Meine Seele wird ein Baum
Und ein Tier und ein Wolkenweben.
Verwandelt und fremd kehrt sie zurück
Und fragt mich. Wie soll ich Antwort geben?

HERMANN HESSE

There Are Times . . .

There are times when a bird sings his note
or the wind stirs dewy twigs that glisten
or a far hound bays with outstretched throat,
I stop in silence long and listen.

Back and back my soul has flown
to a thousand forgotten years away
when the souls of the wind and the bird were my own,
and I, their brother, was as they.

My human soul becomes a tree,
a simple beast, a cloud up high.
How changed my soul returns to me
and questions. . . . How shall I reply?

HERMANN HESSE

Nacht

Ich habe meine Kerze ausgelöscht;
Zum offnen Fenster strömt die Nacht herein,
Umarmt mich sanft und läßt mich ihren Freund
Und ihren Bruder sein.

Wir beide sind am selben Heimweh krank;
Wir senden ahnungsvolle Träume aus
Und reden flüsternd von der alten Zeit
In unsres Vaters Haus.

HERMANN HESSE
Night

I have put out my candlelight;
now bounteous night that knows no end
streams in, caressing, calling me
her brother and her friend.

Ill with a kindred pain, we two
send out our longing dreams to roam,
and whisper of a different time
together in our father's home.

HERMANN HESSE

Allein

Es führen über die Erde
Straßen und Wege viel,
Aber alle haben
Das selbe Ziel.

Du kannst reiten und fahren
Zu zwein und zu drein,
Den letzten Schritt mußt du
Gehen allein.

Drum ist kein Wissen
Noch Können so gut,
Als daß man alles Schwere
Alleine tut.

HERMANN HESSE

Alone

They stretch across this earth-ball:
roads without number or name,
but all are alike:
their goal is the same.

You can ride, you can travel
with a friend of your own;
the final step
you must walk alone.

No wisdom is better
than this, when known:
that every hard thing
is done alone.

HERMANN HESSE

Frühlingstag

Wind im Gesträuch und Vogelpfiff
Und hoch im höchsten süßen Blau
Ein stilles, stolzes Wolkenschiff . . .
Ich träume von einer blonden Frau,
Ich träume von meiner Jugendzeit,
Der hohe Himmel blau und weit,
Ist meiner Sehnsucht Wiege,
Darin ich stillgesinnt
Und selig warm
Mit leisem Summen liege,
So wie in seiner Mutter Arm
Ein Kind.

HERMANN HESSE

Spring Day

Wind in the bush and bird-calls loud,
and high on heaven's bluest pond
a silent-sailing ship of cloud . . .
I dream of a woman, golden-blond;
I dream my youthful time and tide,
and the high heaven, blue and wide,
is like a cradle, wherein I,
cradled in yearning soft and mild
and gently warm,
humming and murmuring lie,
as in its mother's arm:
a child.

HERMANN HESSE

Blume, Baum, Vogel

Bist allein im Leeren,
Glühst einsam, Herz,
Grüßt dich am Abgrund
Dunkle Blume Schmerz.

Reckt seine Äste
Der hohe Baum Leid,
Singt in den Zweigen
Vogel Ewigkeit.

Blume Schmerz ist schweigsam,
Findet kein Wort,
Der Baum wächst bis in die Wolken,
Und der Vogel singt immerfort.

HERMANN HESSE

Flower, Tree, and Bird

Glow, lonely heart,
alone with the hour.
She waits in the shadow:
pain, the dark flower.

Now stretches its branches
suffering's tree,
where sings in the green leaf
the bird, eternity.

Pain's blossom is silent,
her speech is gone.
The tree grows toward heaven,
and the bird sings on.

HERMANN HESSE

Bücher

Alle Bücher dieser Welt
Bringen dir kein Glück,
Doch sie weisen dich geheim
In dich selbst zurück.

Dort ist alles, was du brauchst,
Sonne, Stern und Mond,
Denn das Licht, danach du frugst,
In dir selber wohnt.

Weisheit, die du lang gesucht
In den Bücherein,
Leuchtet jetzt aus jedem Blatt—
Denn nun ist sie dein.

HERMANN HESSE

Books

All the books in all this world
from every nook and shelf
bring no happiness. They turn
you back upon yourself.

Here is every thing you need:
sun and moon and star.
For the clarities you sought,
in yourself they are.

Wisdom longtime vainly wooed
on the bookstore shelf
shimmers now from every page,
reflected from yourself.

HERMANN HESSE

Vergänglichkeit

Vom Baum des Lebens fällt
Mir Blatt um Blatt.
O taumelbunte Welt,
Wie machst du satt,
Wie machst du satt und müd,
Wie machst du trunken!
Was heut noch glüht,
Ist bald versunken.
Bald klirrt der Wind
Über mein braunes Grab,
Über das kleine Kind
Beugt sich die Mutter herab.
Ihre Augen will ich wiedersehn,
Ihr Blick ist mein Stern,
Alles andre mag gehn und verwehn,
Alles stirbt, alles stirbt gern.
Nur die ewige Mutter bleibt,
Von der wir kamen,
Ihr spielender Finger schreibt
In die flüchtige Luft unsre Namen.

HERMANN HESSE

Transition

Leaf after leaf forsakes me
from my life's tree.
How full the world makes me,
the leaves falling free—
how full and how tired,
how gorged and drunken!
What beauty has fired,
burns and is sunken.
The west wind will blow
where my grave lies brown.
On her child below
the mother bends down.
Let me look on her eyes;
her glance is my star.
All else gladly dies,
all, all things that are.
Only she lasts and lingers
from whom we came,
and writes with light fingers
in the winds our name.

HERMANN CLAUDIUS

Mein Kirschbaum

Mein Kirschbaum steht von Blüten weiß umbrämt.
Wie hab' ich meines Menschseins mich geschämt.

Wie war die Gottheit mir erschreckend nah,
da ich den Baum in seiner Blüte sah.

Ich legte beide Hände um die Rinde
und sprach zu Gott: Sei gnädig deinem Kinde.

HERMANN CLAUDIUS
Cherry Tree

In blossoms white my cherry tree stands framed.
That I must be a man made me ashamed.

How frighteningly close God came to me
when I beheld the blossoms and the tree!

I laid both hands about the shining bole
and prayed to God: Have mercy on my soul.

Wasser

Ich gehe abends gern noch an den Fluß,
um mich mit einem Blick daran zu laben.
Die Seele muß vom ewigen Wasser haben,
daß sie so sehr erquickt sein stummer Gruß.

Das Dunkel kriecht aus allen Büschen her
und will den holden Spiegel mir erblinden.
Doch sieh: die allerersten Sterne finden
funkelnd darinnen ihre Wiederkehr.

HERMANN CLAUDIUS
Water

I walk to the river's bank before the night
to stand and watch there for a passing minute.
My soul has something of the water in it
that I should be so lifted by the sight.

The dark creeps out of bush and fern and glen,
as if to make that lovely mirror blind.
But see: the early stars are out and find
themselves below me and shine back again.

HERMANN CLAUDIUS

Der Rosenbusch

Es haben meine wilden Rosen
—erschauernd vor dem Hauch der Nacht—
die windeleichten, lichten, losen
Blüten behutsam zugemacht.

Doch sind sie so voll Licht gesogen,
daß es wie Schleier sie umweht,
und daß die Nacht in scheuem Bogen
am Rosenbusch vorübergeht.

HERMANN CLAUDIUS

Rosebush

Each flower of my wild wood-roses,
atremble at the touch of night,
its wind-light luminous petals closes,
unstirred, fastidious and tight.

And yet they are so drenched in light,
around them veils of whiteness fly;
in tender negligence the night
passes the bush of wild rose by.

HANS CAROSSA

Sternenlied

Morgen werden viele Sterne scheinen,
morgen wirst du nach mir weinen
und ins tote Fenster spähn.
Dann hinauf zum Glanz der Ferne
wirst du fliehn; und tausend Sterne,
all die stillen kleinen Sterne
wirst du durch zwei helle Tränen
groß wie Sonnen zittern sehn.

HANS CAROSSA

Star-Song

Many stars will shine tomorrow;
you will weep for me in sorrow,
through dead windows you will peer.
Then your glance will follow far,
fleeing to the farthest star.
And a thousand little stars
you will see as big as suns,
each through the crystal of a tear.

AGNES MIEGEL

Nachtspuk

Die tote junge Frau im Grab,
sie sprach: „Was klingt nun Tag für Tag
bis in mein stilles Bett hinab
wie Säggeknirsch und Hammerschlag?
Längst fraß das Feuer unser Dorf,
das Gott mit Pest und Tatern schlug.
Nie sah ich Menschen, seit im Torf
der fremde Knecht den Jud erschlug."

Sie schlug zurück ihr Leichentuch
und stieg wie Nebelhauch herauf.
Und harzig quolls wie Brandgeruch,
als sie sich band die Zöpfe auf.
Die Grillen zirpten hell im Gras,
die Frösche quakten dumpf im Rohr,
und überm Tannicht groß und blaß
stieg still und rund der Mond empor.

Das hohe Gras war feucht vom Tau,
sie spürte lächelnd es beim Gehn.
Doch einmal zögerte die Frau
und blieb in tiefem Sinnen stehn.
Vergraben in den Nesseln schier,
versenkt, verwittert aus dem Kraut
ein Roßhaupt sah, des Firstes Zier,
drauf einst der Storch sein Nest gebaut.

Sie ging zum Moore. Wieder blieb
sie stehn. Leis witternd gab sie acht,

AGNES MIEGEL

Ghost

From her grave the dead young woman spoke
and said: "What noise day after day,
like grind of saw and hammer-stroke,
down to my still bed finds its way?
Fire ate our village long before,
that God with pestilence smote and slew.
I saw no men since on the moor
the foreigner struck down the Jew."

She raised her head, her face-cloth fell.
She rose like smoke in the night air.
There was a charred and ashy smell
as she bound up her braided hair.
The crickets in the grass chirped loud,
the frogs croaked in the reeds near-by.
Over the fir copse pale and proud
and still and round the moon crept high.

The spears of grass were damp with dew.
She felt it as she crossed the hill
and smiled, and suddenly she drew
backward and deep in thought stood still.
Buried in nettles where it lay,
a horse-head, long the roof-tree's crest,
in rain and weather rotted away,
where once the stork had built its nest.

Into the moor she turned and stood
to sniff the air, tell if she might

von wo der Wind stand, denn es trieb
wie warmer Herdrauch durch die Nacht.
Da glitt sie eilend durch den Tann
bis zu der Trift. Am Graben stand
ein neu Gehöft. Der Hund schlug an,
und Leinen lag am Rain gespannt.

Zur Rechten lief ein schmaler Pfad
vom Grasplatz bis zum Gärtchen hin.
Zur linken Hand stand junge Saat,
ein schwarzweiß Kätzchen jagte drin.
Durchs Fenster in der Giebelwand
glomm eines späten Lämpchens Schein.
Die tote Frau am Fenster stand
und schauerte und sah hinein.

Ein junges Weib im groben Hemd
ging in der Kammer ab und zu,
und sang—die Worte waren fremd—
schaukelnd ihr kleines Kind zur Ruh.—
Wie Flachs war seines Köpfchens Flaum,
das in den bunten Kissen tief,
die Händchen fingerten im Traum,
mit offnem Mäulchen wohlig schlief.

where lay the wind; the smell of wood
and hearth-smoke drifted through the night.
Quickly she glided through the dark
to the cattle-run. There stood at hand
a new house. Hounds began to bark
and linen on the grass lay spanned.

At the right a path ran straight and neat
to the yard where flower-beds were laid.
On the left hand grew the new green wheat.
In it a spotted kitten played.
Through the window in the wall
a late lamp glowed into the gloom.
The dead one stood there, still and tall,
shuddered and looked into the room.

A slender girl in homespun dressed
passed in the chamber to and fro,
singing her little child to rest.
The words—the dead one did not know.
Like flax his downy round head seemed,
sunk in the chequered pillows deep.
He moved his fingers as he dreamed
with open mouth and fast asleep.

So seltsam ward's der Toten drauß,
als wollt ihr Herz noch einmal gehn.
Die Müde drinnen sah hinaus
und sah den Spuk am Fenster stehn.
Ihr Leib war blaß und spinnwebklar,
altfränkisch ihres Kleides Pracht.
Wie Edelstein in ihrem Haar
lag weiß und blank der Tau der Nacht.

Die Bäuerin schlug ein Kreuz. Das Kind
schrak wimmernd auf. Durchs Wiesental
fuhr kühl ein früher Morgenwind.
Der Hahn rief laut zum erstenmal.
Die Tote bebte, als er schrie,
und sprach: „Wie geht mein Fuß so schwer,
so weit war dieser Weg noch nie—
O Gott, nun komm ich nimmermehr!"

AGNES MIEGEL

It seemed so strange to her dead heart,
as if it now might beat again.
The tired mother gave a start
and saw the ghost at the windowpane.
Her frame was webbed as thin as air
and quaintly styled her gown that blew.
Like jewels that sparkled in her hair
lay bright and white the midnight dew.

The peasant crossed herself. Her child
woke with a cry. Across the hill
a morning wind blew cool and mild.
The cock crowed out now with a will.
The dead one trembled at the cry.
"My step is heavy," she said then.
"The way was never so far—and I—
O God, I'll never come again!"

INA SEIDEL

Ehe

O, daß ich dich fand,
einzig warm und fest,
Hand in meiner Hand,
Hand, die mich nicht läßt!

Meiner Sinne Sinn,
meiner Augen Licht,
wenn ich nächtig bin,
wandelst du dich nicht.

Unsrer Sterne still
ziehn wir morgenwärts,
wie dein Blutstrom will,
meines Herzens Herz.

INA SEIDEL

Marriage

How good that you found me,
hand in my own,
firm grasp around me,
no longer alone!

Mind of my mind,
my sunlight forever;
though I were blind,
you do not waver.

Starward still
our ways do not part;
your blood is my will,
heart of my heart.

GEORG TRAKL

Romanze zur Nacht

Einsamer unterm Sternenzelt
Geht durch die stille Mitternacht.
Der Knab aus Träumen wirr erwacht,
Sein Antlitz grau im Mond verfällt.

Die Närrin weint mit offnem Haar
Am Fenster, das vergittert starrt.
Im Teich vorbei auf süßer Fahrt
Ziehn Liebende sehr wunderbar.

Der Mörder lächelt bleich im Wein,
Die Kranken Todesgrausen packt.
Die Nonne betet wund und nackt
Vor des Heilands Kreuzespein.

Die Mutter leis im Schlafe singt.
Sehr friedlich schaut zur Nacht das Kind
Mit Augen, die ganz wahrhaft sind.
Im Hurenhaus Gelächter klingt.

Beim Talglicht drunt im Kellerloch
Der Tote malt mit weißer Hand
Ein grinsend Schweigen an die Wand.
Der Schläfer flüstert immer noch.

GEORG TRAKL

Nocturne

Beneath the stars a man alone
his pathway through the midnight takes.
Out of wild dreams a boy awakes;
under the moon his face is stone.

With streaming hair a lunatic
weeps at her staring window-bars.
On pale pond-water sewn with stars
lovers are floating past, love-sick.

The murderer drinks his wine wide-eyed.
Invalids shake with fear of death.
A nun prays nude with bated breath
before the saviour crucified.

A sleeping mother sways and sings
Her child looks toward the moon's soft light
with eyes still truth-filled in the night.
Out of the whorehouse laughter rings.

By candle in the cellar deep
from fingers of the freshly dead
on walls a grinning hush is spread.
The sleeper whispers in his sleep.

ERNST WIECHERT

Ein Kind hat geweint

Wenn die Uhren schlagen um die halbe Nacht,
Bin ich erwacht,
Aus den Wäldern der Träume ausgestoßen
Und mit den bloßen Füßen ins Schweigen gestellt,
Wenn von den großen Zeigern die Stille fällt.
Ich sitze und lausche . . . was war es doch?
Es hat doch leise an die Wand gepocht?
Es hat doch leise mein Herz angerührt?
Es hat sich doch bis in meine Träume verirrt?
Es hat doch . . . es hat doch geweint in der Nacht,
Und davon bin ich so furchtbar erwacht?
Über den Garten geht leise der Wind.

Die Bäume sind wach in der blauen Welt,
Aus der ein Stern nach dem andern fällt,
Und das Haus ist wach und die Wände klopfen,
Und über die Treppen fällt es in Tropfen . . .
Und nun weiß ich: es war ein Kind.
Ein Kind hat geweint um die halbe Nacht,
Und davon bin ich so furchtbar erwacht.
Und nun hör ich es klagen aus fremden Gärten,
Und wo ein Licht noch im Dunkel scheint,
Da hat es geweint.
Es wandert und irrt auf ziellosen Fährten.
Nun steht es an meines Bettes Rand,
Nun tastet es jammernd hinter der Wand,
Nun steht es am Waldrand im Mondenschein,
Und immer, immer ist es allein.

ERNST WIECHERT

A Child Cried at Night

Half through the night at a deep clock-stroke
on a sudden I woke,
banished out of my dreams' dark wood,
barefoot I stood in the hush alone
when from great clock-hands silence is thrown.
I sit and listen: did something tick
in the wall, deep under plaster and brick?
Did something brush my heart—or the beams?
Did something wander into my dreams?
Or did something . . . something cried in the night
that woke me and filled me so with fright.
Over the garden the wind blows mild.

The trees are awake in that blue world.
Star after star is downward hurled.
And the house is awake and the four walls quiver
and the long stairs drizzle and drip and shiver.
And now I know: it was a child.
A child cried out, half through the night,
and I awoke then, bathed in fright.
And I hear it whine in strangers' homes,
and where a light pushes the dark aside;
there it cried.
Aimlessly it wanders and roams;
now it stands by my pillow's edge;
now it weeps and gropes by the window ledge;
now it stops by the woods in the moon to moan,
and always, always it's alone.

Ich hebe die Hände: „Du Kind . . . o du Kind!"
Aber wieder geht nur leise über den Garten der Wind.
Und plötzlich weiß ich, zu Qual versteint:
Das Kind hat in meinem H e r z e n geweint.

Tief an den Wurzeln des Lebensbaumes,
Wo das Blut mir bitter vor Sehnsucht rinnt,
Da kauert das Kind,
Und klopft mich aus dumpfem Leben ans Licht,
Und flüstert schmerzlich: „G e d e n k s t d u
                                    denn nicht?"

I lift my hands: "You child—O you child!"
But again the wind in the garden blows warm and mild.
Then I know, with pain and horror petrified:
It's *in my heart* the child has cried.

Down at the roots that once were I,
where my blood with longing runs bitter and dry,
there cowers the child and shields a dying ember
and whispers in sorrow to me: "Don't you remember?"

HEINRICH LERSCH

Brüder

Es lag schon lang ein Toter vor unserm Drahtverhau,
die Sonne auf ihn glühte, ihn kühlte Wind und Tau.

Ich sah ihm alle Tage in sein Gesicht hinein,
und immer fühlt' ich's fester: Er muß mein Bruder sein.

Ich sah in allen Stunden, wie er so vor mir lag,
und hörte seine Stimme aus frohem Friedenstag.

Oft in der Nacht ein Weinen, das aus dem Schlaf mich trieb,
mein Bruder, lieber Bruder—hast du mich nicht mehr lieb?

Bis ich, trotz aller Kugeln, zur Nacht mich ihm genaht
und ihn geholt.—Begraben:—Ein fremder Kamerad.

Es irrten meine Augen.—Mein Herz, du irrst dich nicht;
es hat ein jeder Toter des Bruders Angesicht.

HEINRICH LERSCH

Brothers

Before our barbed and tangled wire, long time a dead man lay;
the beating sun, the cooling wind each had with him its way.

Those many days I stood hard by and looked into his face
and wondered more and more: How comes my brother to this
    place?

I saw at every hour of day his body on the ground,
and out of happy days of peace I heard his soft voice sound.

Often at night a weeping woke and would not let me be:
My brother, my dear brother, where is your love for me?

Until, despite the bullets there, by night my way I found
and brought him back and buried him: a comrade from beyond.

My eyes mistook him, yet my heart knew him in that dark place.
For there is never a dead man but has my brother's face.

FRANZ WERFEL

Ich bin ein erwachsener Mensch

Ich hab' so ein Verlangen
Nach Mitleid und nach Zärtlichtun.
Ich möchte nun
Im Bette liegen stundenlang,
So kindergut, so fieberkrank
Und liebe Hände langen.

                Ich hab' so ein Verlangen.

Kein Mensch will mich bewachen,
Und niemand hätschelt mich und summt.
Ach, alle Freundlichkeit verstummt,
Und keine kleine Lampe brennt,
Und niemand der mich Bubi nennt,
Kein Spielzeug, und kein Lachen.

Wer streichelt meine Wangen?

                Ich hab' so ein Verlangen.

FRANZ WERFEL

I Am a Grown Man

I have oh such a yearning
for pity and for tenderness.
I'd like to rest
for hours in bed, as if forever,
as children rest when sick with fever,
hold hands that soothe the burning.
   I have oh such a yearning.

There's none alive who will look after
or baby me and rock and hum.
All friendliness grows dull and dumb.
And there is no small lamp alight
and none to call me boy tonight,
no plaything and no laughter.

Who strokes my brow that's burning?
   I have oh such a yearning.

JOSEF WEINHEBER

Unbekannte Frau

Woher du kommst, ich weiß es nicht.
Im Himmel hoch die Wolke zieht.
Vom Baume tropft ein Morgenlied.
Die Blüten schneien weiß und dicht.

Wer bist du, unbekannte Frau?
Mittäglich schweigt ein voller Tag.
Die Schlange gleißt im Buchenschlag.
Fern schläft ein Berg im satten Blau.

Dein Schicksal rührt mich dunkel an.
Der Abend deckt die Quellen zu.
Aus Purpurgründen rauscht die Ruh.
Ob wir uns vordem einmal sahn?

Es trinkt die Nacht dein Angesicht.
Ich habe wohl sehr lang geträumt?
Ein letzter Bord den Himmel säumt:
Du schwindest, gehst—und bist Gedicht.

JOSEF WEINHEBER

Unknown Woman

Whence you have come, it puzzles me.
A cloud floats past on heaven's height.
Blossoms are snowing thick and white.
A morning song drips from the tree.

Who are you, woman all unknown?
On us the noonday silence drops.
The snake glints in the beechwood copse.
The hill sleeps heavy and alone.

You move me in unfathomed ways.
The spring's dusk covers, twilight swallows.
Quiet comes up from purple hollows.
Did our paths meet in other days?

Now night drinks up your face. Night drains
the dream; was its slow dreamer I?
One little border frames the sky.
You vanish—and a verse remains.

MAX BARTHEL

Der Pflug

Es liegt ein Feld mit Granaten besät,
da hat der Krieg mit donnernden Schlägen gemäht,
hat die Erde mit Garben mit Menschen bedeckt
und ist dann in weitere Fernen geschreckt.

Nur ein Pflug, wie ihn der Bauer verließ,
als ihn der Wind des Todes anblies,
steht ruhig im Feld, zur Arbeit bereit,
als käme schon morgen die friedliche Zeit.

Als käme schon morgen das Ende der Not,
als grüne schon morgen das heilige Brot,
als blühe, was der Tag gestern zerschlug . . .
Ruhig wartet im Feld der Pflug.

MAX BARTHEL

The Plow

There is a field sown with mines in rows,
where war made harvest with thundering blows.
He covered the ground with sheaves of men
and marched to further harvesting then.

Only a plow, abandoned that day
when the wind of death blew the ploughman away,
stands in the field and ready for toil,
as though new dawn brought peace to the soil.

As though the new day would end the dread
and sprout the holy harvest of bread,
and what war reddened were greening now . . .
Calmly it waits in the field: the plow.

ALBRECHT HAUSHOFER

In Fesseln

(„MOABITER SONETTE")

Für den, der nächtlich in ihr schlafen soll,
so kahl die Zelle schien, so reich an Leben
sind ihre Wände. Schuld und Schicksal weben
mit grauen Schleiern ihr Gewölbe voll.

Von allem Leid, das diesen Bau erfüllt,
ist unter Mauerwerk und Eisengittern
ein Hauch lebendig, ein geheimes Zittern,
das andrer Seelen tiefe Not enthüllt.

Ich bin der erste nicht in diesem Raum,
in dessen Handgelenk die Fessel schneidet,
an dessen Gram sich fremder Wille weidet.

Der Schlaf wird Wachen wie das Wachen Traum.
Indem ich lausche, spür ich durch die Wände
das Beben vieler brüderlicher Hände.

ALBRECHT HAUSHOFER

In Chains

("SONNETS FROM MOABITE PRISON")

Bare though it seemed at first, this close-built cell
when nightly sleep might knit care's raveled sleeve,
its walls are teeming. Guilt and a sure fate weave
grey veils across the vaults where I must dwell.

Out of the sufferings that fill these blocks
of stone and mortar, brick and iron grating,
one secret breath is living, shaking, waiting:
the pain of soul that strains and bursts all locks.

For I am not the first to pace this square,
the first whose wrist the angry fetters bite,
the first whose pain is fodder for strange spite.

My sleep is waking, waking is nightmare.
And while I listen, through the dead stone shudders
the trembling of the hands of many brothers.

ALBRECHT HAUSHOFER

Rattenzug

(,,MOABITER SONETTE")

Ein Heer von grauen Ratten frißt im Land.
Sie nähern sich dem Strom in wildem Drängen.
Voraus ein Pfeifer, der mit irren Klängen
zu wunderlichen Zuckungen sie band.

So ließen sie die Speicher voll Getreide—
was zögern wollte, wurde mitgerissen,
was widerstrebte, blindlings totgebissen—
so zogen sie zum Strom, der Flur zuleide . . .

Sie wittern in dem Brausen Blut und Fleisch,
verlockender und wilder wird der Klang—
sie stürzen schon hinab den Uferhang— —

ein schriller Pfiff—ein gellendes Gekreisch:
Der irre Laut ersäuft im Stromgebraus . . .
die Ratten treiben tot ins Meer hinaus . . .

ALBRECHT HAUSHOFER

The Rats

("SONNETS FROM MOABITE PRISON")

An army of grey rats devours our land,
throngs toward the river, ravenous and bold.
And see the madcap piper who can hold
rats bound in spasm by his artful hand!

The bins of yellow grain were full to bursting;
the few that straggled there were borne along;
the strugglers, fewer, perished in the throng.
They crush the fields, rush to the river, thirsting.

They catch the scent of blood, deep in the stream.
The piper's music rings more wild, more teasing;
down muddy shores they plunge, squealing and wheezing.

One whistle shrill—one single piercing scream:
the crazy music drowns in the loud commotion, . . .
the dead rats drive downstream and toward the ocean.

ULRICH BECHER

Abendländers Gelübd

Wir wollen tun,
nicht ruhn,
Und übern Totenfluß, den Rhein,
soll eine starke Brücke sein,
auf der die Heerscharen,
die jubelnden,
die waffenlosen,
aus alter Bibelpost
zu Fleisch geworden,
lächelnd herfahren
von Süd nach Norden,
aus West zu Ost.
Mein Tal, dein Tal,
mein Haus, dein Haus,
mein Kind, dein Kind,
im fremden Mondgefahl,
im Surrn der Fledermaus,
im Abendflüsterwind
sollt ihr zu Frieden ruhn.
Wir wollen tun.

ULRICH BECHER

Vow of the European

Let deeds be our quest,
not rest.
And over the Rhine, Death's river,
a strong bridge be forever,
where march the mighty hosts of man
with gladness,
the weaponless,
as the great Book's promise ran,
now bodied forth,
as to a feast,
from south to north,
from west to east.
My vale, thy vale,
my roof, thy roof,
my child, thy child,
in the moonlight pale,
in whir of bat aloof,
in lisp of night-wind mild,
all, all shall find rest.
Let deeds be our quest.

HANS EGON HOLTHUSEN

Hingabe

Daß man am Tage auf den Traum verzichte!
Du feines Herzglas von erlesnem Schliff,
Auf Wein gefaßt und schäumende Gesichte:
Gemeines Wasser sei dir Inbegriff.

Leih deiner Sehnsucht Prunk dem Unscheinbaren,
Geh jeden Tag auf eine Kummerstatt,
Gewöhn dich an den Wohlgeschmack des Wahren,
Zu dem dich keine Lust gestachelt hat.

Belausche die Verdrießlichen und Schalen,
Die Armen, Kümmerlichen, Teppichklopfer,
Und laß von ihrem Atem dich bestrahlen.

Du schöne Wolke, schweifendes Gespinst,
O bringe dich als Niederschlag zum Opfer,
Tu einem Kraut den ungerühmten Dienst.

Sacrifice

By day forget your dream, renounce all dreaming!
Heart's vessel, choicely cut of crystal true,
visioned for wine and fashioned for its gleaming,
let common water be the blood in you.

Bend your bright yearning to simplicity,
seek out Grief's daily haunts and go to her.
Acquire the flavor of reality
toward which no sharp desire has given spur.

Eavesdrop the shallow and the dispossessed,
the worried poor, rutted routine's vast nation;
by their hot breath let your brow be caressed.

And lovely cloud, spun by the wind's wild speed,
give all yourself as a precipitation,
bring nameless service to a common weed.

HANS EGON HOLTHUSEN

Es War Mein Blut

(AUS: „KLAGE UM DEN BRUDER")

Es war mein Blut, das sich aus dir ergossen.
Nun ist mir alles fremd. Nun gehst du tot
In dieses Dasein ein. So sei mein Brot
Hinfort nicht ohne deinen Tod genossen.

Mein Herz fühlt aus den Angeln sich gehoben
Und sieht die Dinge schwindlig und verändert.
Die Blumen sind mit Todeslicht gerändert,
Und alle Horizonte sind verschoben.

O furchtbar, einen Bruder zu besitzen
Und einmal nur—dies Kreuz ward uns gesetzt—
Berühren dürfen mit den Fingerspitzen!

Ein kleiner Ruck der Zeit hat dich getroffen,
Ein bloßer Lidschlag zwischen jetzt und jetzt,
Und meine Arme bleiben ewig offen.

HANS EGON HOLTHUSEN
It Was My Blood
(FROM "LAMENT FOR MY BROTHER")

It was my blood that from you spilt and wasted.
Now all is strange to me. Now you sink dead,
sink into this existence. Let my bread,
without your death in it, no more be tasted.

My heart is slanted on its hinges, listing,
seeing things dizzied, out of all proper order.
Each flower is edged with deathlight at its border,
and all horizons are awry and twisting.

How terrible, to love a brother much
and know our fate that only would allow
the fingertips a single hurried touch!

How lastingly one brush of Time can sever,
one little lid-beat between now and now,
and my two arms are open here forever.